The Making of a Champion

A Baseball All-Star

Heinemann Library
Chicago, Illinois

Brendan January

Customer Service   888–454–2279
Visit our website at www.heinemannlibrary.com

Editorial: Geoff Barker, Rebecca Hunter and Jennifer Huston
Design: Keith Williams
Illustrations: Peter Bull
Picture Research: Rachel Tisdale
Production: John Nelson

Originated by Ambassador Litho Ltd
Printed in China by WKT Company Limited.

09 08 07 06 05
10 9 8 7 6 5 4 3 2 1

Library of Congress Cataloging-in-Publication Data
January, Brendan, 1972-
A baseball all-star / Brendan January.
p. cm. -- (The making of a champion)
Includes bibliographical references and index.
ISBN 1-4034-5362-4 (library binding-hardcover) -- ISBN 1-4034-5546-5 (pbk.)
1. Baseball--Juvenile literature. I. Title. II. Series.
GV867.5.J26 2004
796.357--dc22
2004003862
                              2003011621

Acknowledgments
The author and publisher are grateful to the following for permission to reproduce copyright
material:
Corbis pp **9** (Bettman), **10** (Joseph Sohm), **11** bottom (Annie Griffiths), **13** top & **21** top
(Bettman), **24** (Lon Dematteis), **36** (Layne Kennedy), **38** (Jeff Topping), **40** (Reuters); Empics
pp **5**, **12**, **19**, **20**, **33 bottom**; Getty Images pp **4** (Brian Bahr), **6**, **7 top**, **8** (Elsa), **11 top**
(Andy Lyons), **13 bottom** (Doug Pensinger), **14** (Jonathan Daniel), **15** (Otto Greule), **16**
(Jeff Gross), **17** (Doug Pensinger), **18** (Jamie Squire), **21 bottom** (Jonathan Daniel), **22**
(Otto Greule), **23** (Ezra Shaw), **25 top**, **25 bottom** (Brian Bahr), **26** (Otto Greule), **27**
(Eliot J Schechter), **28** (Matthew Stockman), **29 top** (Otto Greule), **29 bottom** (Jonathan
Daniel), **30** (Doug Pensinger), **31** (Otto Greule), **32** (Stephen Dunn), **33 top** (Jonathan
Daniel), **34** (Matthew Stockman), **35 top** (Ezra Shaw), **35 bottom** (Doug Pensinger),
37 top (Chris Hondros), **37 bottom** (Scott Halleran), **39** (Jonathan Daniel), **41** & **42**
(Jed Jacobsohn), **43** (Eliot J Schechter).

Cover photograph reproduced with permission of Reuters/Corbis.

Contents

Introducing baseball

On any night in the summer, the crack of a bat meeting a baseball can be heard across three continents. It can be on a city block in Boston, or a sand lot in the Dominican Republic, or a sleek stadium in Tokyo before thousands of fans. Each place may be vastly different, but each game has the same look and feel— a bat, a ball, a field of bases, and nine players.

Baseball is a sport of precise movements performed at blurring speed— scooping up a skipping ground ball, throwing a 95 m.p.h. fastball, adjusting a swing to hit a pitch. For this reason, it is a sport of endless repetition. Each player must spend hours repeating the same drills to make catching, swinging, and throwing as fluid as possible. Only when these basic movements are mastered can a player make the necessary adjustments during a game.

The mental game

Baseball is also a game of pauses and delays—between each pitch, after a play, between innings. There are no clocks to race against. During these moments, when nothing seems to be happening, the most important part of the game is being played—the mental game. Each player uses these pauses to make endless calculations, to make critical adjustments, and to plan how best to make the next play. It is this aspect of the game, often lost on the casual observer, that makes baseball so enjoyable to fans. One pitcher called baseball a "game of chess played at 90 miles per hour."

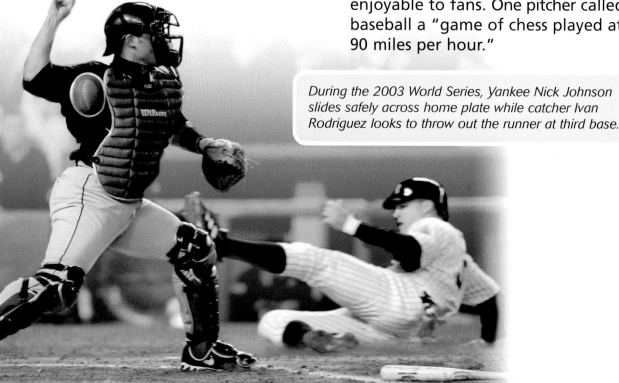

During the 2003 World Series, Yankee Nick Johnson slides safely across home plate while catcher Ivan Rodriguez looks to throw out the runner at third base.

Excitement

Once the pauses are over, baseball explodes with speed, power, and excitement. It can be a throw to home plate to cut down a sliding runner. It can be a strikeout that ends the inning. It can be a powerful swing that connects perfectly, knocking the ball in a high arc that lands over the fence in a colorful frenzy of cheering fans.

Major League diversity

Once the domain of U.S. players, Major League Baseball is now played by more people from around the world than ever before. In 2003, nearly one-third of all Major Leaguers were from another country, including ten percent from the Dominican Republic alone. Fans are also treated to players from countries such as Mexico, Venezuela, Canada, Japan, South Korea, and

Major League island

The tiny island country of the Dominican Republic has produced some of Major League baseball's best players, including Sammy Sosa of the Chicago Cubs, Albert Pujols *(above)* of the St. Louis Cardinals, and Pedro Martinez of the Boston Red Sox. Baseball started in the Dominican Republic in the 1870s. Cubans, who had learned the game from American sailors, fled to the Dominican Republic during a ten-year war. They brought baseball with them. The Dominicans play baseball with fanaticism all year round.

Australia. The trend will continue. Nearly half of the more than 6,000 players in the minor leagues today were born outside the United States.

Baseball: A sport's beginnings

Baseball first emerged in the United States in the mid-1800s. By end of the century, leagues had been formed and regulations written down. It has been played by the same basic rules ever since, though the style has changed enormously. Baseball was not only popular in the United States, the sport spread to Latin America and Japan in the late 1800s and early 1900s, where it was picked up with enthusiasm.

Base ball

Like most things today called American, baseball had its origins in other countries. British settlers brought ball and stick games called cricket and rounders to North America. Variations of these games spread with names such as "old cat," "sting ball," "round ball," and "base ball." In 1803, American explorers taught a Native American tribe "the game of base." The game grew popular, especially as more people began to live in crowded cities. Adults and children were urged to leave the city streets to exercise and play in the fresh air on a grassy field. The first official baseball game was held in Hoboken, New Jersey, in 1846, between two New York teams. Over the next decades, leagues sprang up all over the Northeast.

Kids didn't always need a grassy field to play baseball. Here, a young pitcher winds up in a city alley in the early 1900s.

The Negro leagues

Before African Americans were allowed to play in the Major Leagues in the late 1940s, they played in separate leagues with 140-game seasons and a World Series. Some of baseball's greatest stars played in those leagues, most notably pitcher Satchel Paige. Paige became the oldest rookie in Major League baseball history when he pitched his first game for the Cleveland Indians at age 39.

Baseball in different times and cultures

The sport has been played in many different styles and by different people. In the early 1900s, the ball was heavier and hitters focused on driving ground balls and line drives through the infield. This changed in the 1920s, when ballparks built fences. The ball was also stitched tighter, allowing it to be hit further. Babe Ruth hit a massive number of home runs. At that time, African Americans, who were forced to play in separate leagues, developed a game of strategy and speed. This type of game grew popular in Latin America, where Spanish-speaking players competed with enormous grace. The Japanese picked up baseball in the 1870s from U.S. schoolteachers and loved its emphasis on teamwork. During World War II (1939–1945), most men joined the armed forces. Baseball was kept alive by women, who played in the All-American Girls Professional Baseball League.

The field

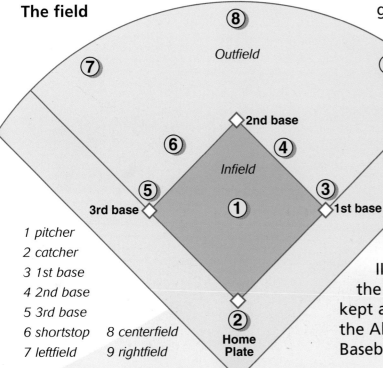

1 pitcher
2 catcher
3 1st base
4 2nd base
5 3rd base
6 shortstop
7 leftfield
8 centerfield
9 rightfield

Little League

Young baseball players will most likely learn the sport in Little League, which has programs in every state and in 104 countries. Little League is affiliated with USA Baseball, which is the national governing body of U.S. amateur baseball. More than two million young people play Little League each year. Leagues for girls began in 1974.

Differences between Little League and professional baseball

Though Little League has virtually the same rules as Major League baseball, there are important differences. Most of these concern the size of the field, which is smaller than those used at the high school and Major League levels. The distance between the bases is 60 feet, rather than the traditional 90 feet. Home run fences are also much closer than in Major League ballparks.

Little League games usually last six innings, rather than nine. The object of Little League is to ensure that young players learn the fundamentals of the sport and have a good time. Coaches are required to play all their players, regardless of ability. To prevent arm injuries, the league also limits the number of innings a pitcher can pitch.

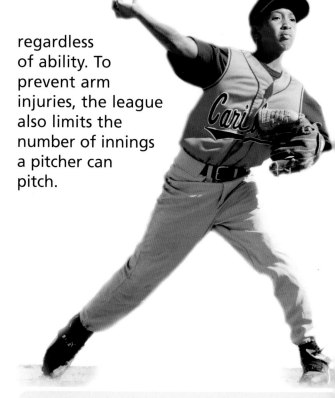

A young player fires the ball to a teammate during the Little League World Series 2003.

Little League World Series fact

The first Little League World Series was won in 1947 by the Maynard Midgets of Williamsport, Pennsylvania. Since then the Little League World Series has expanded to include teams from around the world. In 1957, the first year that teams from outside the United States were allowed to participate in it, a Mexican team from Monterey won the World Series. Ten years later, a team from West Tokyo, Japan, won the coveted game. By this time, the Little League World Series was being broadcast on ABC television. In 2001, George W. Bush became the first U.S. president to visit the Little League World Series.

History of Little League

In the summer of 1938, Carl E. Stotz (right) organized a baseball game for the neighborhood children in Williamsport, Pennsylvania. He shortened the distance between bases to 60 feet and made the game 6 innings long. Next year, Stotz convinced three local businesses to contribute money for a new league. They donated $30, enough to buy uniforms named after the businesses—Lycoming Dairy, Lundy Lumber, and Jumbo Pretzel. Little League was born. The games were played in a vacant lot. Within 10 years, Stotz's model had expanded to 307 leagues located throughout the country. It soon spread to more than 104 countries. Today, Little League is played with the same rules and the same emphasis on fun and teamwork. New York Yankee Hall of Fame catcher Yogi Berra said, "If a kid isn't having fun in Little League, he shouldn't be in it."

Other youth leagues

Many local leagues, however, are not run by Little League. They may use slightly different rules or are more openly competitive. It is important for each young player to look closely at available leagues and select one that is a good match.

The Babe Ruth League, with 800,000 players, is a respected organization with clubs throughout the United States. Dixie Baseball, a southern organization, has 400,000 players in 11 states. The Amateur Athletic Union (AAU) is regarded as one of the most competitive leagues. Teams routinely travel outside their towns to play other clubs.

The importance of starting young

Playing in a youth league is critical for young baseball players. It will be their first experience of baseball as a team sport and their first chance to compete with their peers. An estimated 80 percent of today's Major League baseball players participated in Little League.

Nomar Garciaparra, the star shortstop for the Boston Red Sox and one of the best hitters in baseball, remembered enjoying his time in a youth league, but also taking it seriously. "Even in my first year, 'No-Nonsense' was my nickname," he recalled. "I never fooled around, not even at five years old. Kids were throwing their gloves around, joking around. But I was always focused. I'd get mad if the other guys fooled around."

After Little League

Young baseball players can play Little League until they reach the age of eighteen. After Little League, some players play for their high school team, with many also signing up for a summer league. After high school, college teams and the minor leagues are the next steps. All of these stages are crucial for a player's development.

In high school baseball, the quality of the program, coaching, and competition can vary dramatically. High school is an important time for any young athlete because the young adult body is growing and changing. Young players may feel awkward or slower as their body grows rapidly. This is the time, however, when players should intensify their efforts to master the skills of baseball. They must learn to harness their new strength and size for the delicate precision required by the sport.

Randy Johnson of the Arizona Diamondbacks, one of the best pitchers today, struggled in high school as his body grew into a massive six-foot, ten-inch frame. Throwing a hard fastball was not the problem. Throwing it to a pinpoint spot was. "If you've been blessed with a good fastball, you must learn how to throw it for strikes. It took me a lot longer than most to figure out how to harness the power of this pitch," he said.

Johnson also urged young pitchers to start thinking like a big league pitcher. "Think of high school as the time to get to know your strengths and weaknesses as a pitcher," he said. "Take the initiative to learn about hitters and how they operate."

The minor leagues

Almost all young prospects must play in the minor leagues, which are located around the country and organized in three levels, A, AA, and AAA. A is the lowest league. AAA is just below the Major Leagues, and Major League players often play in the league to recover from an injury or sharpen their skills. The leagues get more competitive and difficult the higher up a player goes. Here the Knoxville Smokies play a minor league game against the Greenville Braves in Knoxville, Tennessee.

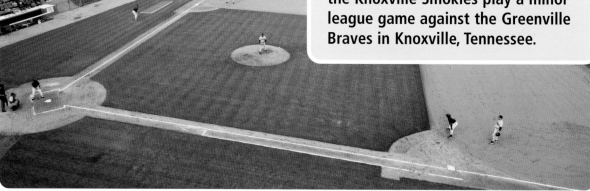

Rule IV draft

High school and college players can be drafted into the major leagues every year through the Rule IV draft. Each team gets one pick per round. Usually, the best prospects are picked first, though getting picked high does not mean the player will be successful. One-third of first round picks never play a single inning of Major League baseball. Several of today's stars were unobserved or ignored. Mike Piazza, the power-hitting catcher for the New York Mets, was not picked until the 62nd round. Houston Astros pitcher Andy Pettite, one of the best left-handed pitchers today, was not picked until the 22nd round.

As his teammates stand and watch, a runner slides across home plate, beating the throw.

High school is an essential time for a young player's development. Here, high school players sit on a dugout bench and watch a game.

Equipment

Using good equipment is essential for a young player both to enjoy the sport and to develop his or her skills properly. It does not take much equipment to play pick-up baseball: a bat, a ball, and some open space. To play in a league, however, each player should be prepared to buy a mitt and a pair of cleats. Most of the other equipment—uniforms, bats, helmets, and catching gear—is provided by the team. No catcher should practice without full safety gear and no hitter should step into a batter's box without a helmet.

A good mitt

The most important piece of equipment for a young player is their mitt, or glove. The young player must "break in" the mitt by using oil and repeated use. Some care should be taken in buying a leather mitt. A poorly constructed mitt, made out of plastic or some other cheap material, will lower the young player's confidence. Facing a line drive or a fly ball can be scary enough, but it is no fun when the player is worried they will make an error or injure their hand.

This infielder slaps the tag on a sliding runner.

Athletic shoes

Cleats, or spikes, are important, especially since the playing conditions vary on different fields. Baseball is also traditionally played through light rain showers without lightning. Infields can be muddy or pocked with rain puddles. A player should be ready to play on slippery, wet grass. An infielder charging a ground ball or an outfielder chasing down a fly ball know the importance of good cleats. An entire game can be lost if a fielder slips at the wrong time.

Swinging the bat

Professional baseball players urge young players to practice batting everyday, even if the player is not hitting a ball. Harmon Killebrew, Hall of Famer from the Minnesota Twins, said getting used to just hitting things helped develop hand-eye coordination and arm strength. Killebrew said he would hit the flowers off his mother's rosebush, pretending they were pitches at different levels. "I don't believe in beating rose bushes with a bat, but I do believe that regular swinging of the bat helps you get the feel of it and learn to control it".

Bat

Players should consider buying a baseball bat. Aluminum bats, because they are far more durable than wooden bats, are used at most levels below the minor leagues. More important, owning a bat encourages a player to continue swinging outside of practice.

A Major League catcher would never play in a game without full equipment—helmet, face mask, chest protector, and shin guards.

Batting

Batting requires patience, technique, and good habits. Young players should learn good habits of hitting early, such as the proper stance and how to swing.

Finding the right bat

The first rule of hitting is to get a bat that feels comfortable in your hands. Bats come in different sizes. Young players should pick each one up and give it a swing. They should not try to impress teammates by swinging a bat that is too heavy or too long. Their play at the plate will suffer. If necessary, they should choke up— hold the bat higher up the barrel. A bat that feels comfortable allows the batter to swing with control and power.

Finding the right stance

The batting stance should be the one that is most comfortable. Movements, such as swaying or rocking the bat, are not important. Keep it simple. The young hitter should concentrate on the moment of the swing. The hands should be "cocked," holding the bat up and ready to swing. The hitter should stride forward and land softly, maintaining his or her balance.

Alex Rodriguez, who now plays for the New York Yankees, looks comfortable and poised as he awaits the next pitch.

Seeing the ball and swinging

As the ball hurtles toward the batter, he or she should stay focused. Tony Gwynn has one of the most impressive hitting records in baseball history—he hit more than .300 for 19 straight seasons. He claims there is a special trick that helps him focus. He looks at the team logo on the pitcher's hat. When the pitcher starts to throw, Gwynn focuses on the point where the pitcher will release the ball. That way, Gwynn sees the pitch from the moment it begins, and he can adjust to hit it.

Hitters should not try to get a tremendous hit every time they bat. After all, even the best hitters are successful only 30 percent of the time. Rather, they should concentrate on doing the little things correctly—standing properly, seeing the ball, and taking good swings. When batters do this, the hits will come.

The wiffle ball practice drill

Tony Gwynn said a young hitter can improve his or her swing dramatically by hitting a wiffle ball off of a batting tee. He calls it a secret weapon. When you "hit the wiffle ball correctly, you should hear air whooshing through the holes as it flies through the air, not that whinier spinning sound." Gwynn uses the tee to practice hitting over different parts of the plate, inside, down the middle, and outside.

Hitting for the cycle fact

One of the most difficult feats for a hitter is to hit "for the cycle." This means that the batter hits a single, a double, a triple, and a home run in a single game. A recent hitter to accomplish this was Philadelphia Phillie David Bell on June 28, 2004.

Throwing

Throwing a baseball appears so simple that many young players don't learn to do it properly. The act, however, is basic to the sport. A good throw is the basis of pitching and fielding. Moreover, each position requires a different style of throw. An infielder must be able to flip the ball a few feet precisely but lightly; an outfielder must fire the ball to a catcher's glove several hundred feet away.

A good grip is needed to throw a baseball properly. Try to put your fingers so they cross over the seams. The thrower should step into the throw and throw overhand. If possible, the player should also point his or her shoe towards the target. Throws should be firm, but not too strong or the ball may sail over the target. Another common error to avoid is aiming. Throwing is a very simple act, and thinking about it often leads to mistakes.

Different positions

Each position requires different kinds of throws. When outfielders catch a ball and need to make a throw to the plate, they often do what is called a crow hop. After catching the ball, the outfielder steps lightly with his or her back foot and hops forward.

The momentum puts more power behind the throw. The ball should be kept low. A ball thrown in a high arc takes longer to reach its target.

Dodgers outfielder Jeremy Burnitz fields a baseball and throws it to the infield. Notice his fingers are gripping the ball across the seams, which will give him more power and accuracy.

Infielders require different throwing styles, mostly because they throw different distances. The third baseman must have a powerful arm to fire the ball across the infield to first base. Second basemen can throw more lightly. Shortstops must be able to adjust. They may have to throw out a runner from "deep in the hole"—that means chasing down a ground ball to the third base side. And they must be able to delicately flip the ball to the second baseman to begin a double play.

Cal Ripken Jr.'s throwing style

Cal Ripken Jr., who played shortstop for the Baltimore Orioles between 1981 and 2001, learned to use just enough strength to throw a runner out, thereby sparing his arm extra fatigue and injury. He didn't throw overhand—he dropped his arm to a "3/4" position. This allowed him to throw accurately but without too much strain. Ripken developed his throw while in the minor leagues because he made too many throwing errors. "I started to understand control, and I came up with [a] three-quarters flip," he said. "I realized I could get the ball to first base quickly enough without throwing a thousand miles per hour, and I'd save my arm and have more control."

Pitching

The pitcher holds the ball at the beginning of each play and sets the game in motion. He or she must use power and precision to throw the ball 60 feet 6 inches to an exact spot. A mistake can lose the game. The pitcher must also be mentally strong, using a choice of location and different speeds to cause the hitter to make an out.

Start with location

Little League pitchers should worry less about throwing pitches that curve or slide, called breaking pitches, and more about throwing with accuracy. Good pitching requires location, location, and location. It is no use throwing hard or fancy if a pitcher cannot control where the ball is landing. Every young pitcher must develop a steady, accurate fastball.

The four-seam and two-seam fastball

The two-seam fastball has more movement than a four-seam fastball and generally tails downward. It is a good strikeout pitch. The four-seam fastball is more accurate and may rise a little. It is a good pitch to get a pop up.

Leo Mazzone's tips for young pitchers

Leo Mazzone coaches one of the most successful pitching staffs in baseball history—the Atlanta Braves. Mazzone said that pitching "is a matter of learning how to put some feel and touch on the ball." He encourages young pitchers to throw every day and to avoid fooling around during practice. "The key is to be consistent and to throw every day," he said. He advises young pitchers to experiment during these practices. They should try spins and rotations to make the ball weave or break. "You'd be surprised how much you can learn just by throwing the ball and trying to do different things with your pitches."

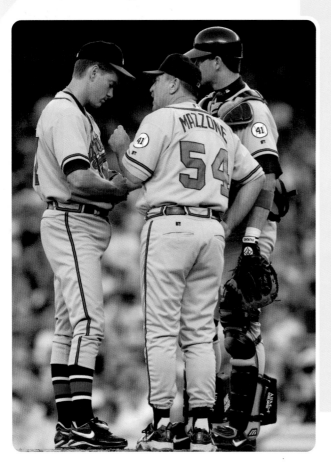

To throw the four-seam fastball, the pitcher grips the ball with his or her first two fingers and thumb across the horseshoe shape of the ridges *(see below)*. The end of the fingers should rest on the ridges. When the pitcher throws, he snaps the ridges, creating backspin.

backward. To throw a "circle change," the pitcher holds the ball deep in his or her palm, with the index finger in a circle on the side of the ball. The middle and ring fingers should be along the seams and the pinkie on the other side of the ball *(see below)*.

Four-seam fast ball *Two-seam fast ball* *Change-up* *Curve ball*

To throw the two-seam fastball, he or she positions the two fingers along the ridges *(see above)*. This will cause the ball to sink as it approaches the plate.

Off-speed and breaking pitches

When the young pitcher has a good, accurate fastball, he or she can start working on developing off-speed and breaking pitches change-ups—and curves.

The change-up fools the batter into believing the pitch is coming faster than it is. The pitcher uses the same arm speed and the same location, but the pitch appears to abruptly slow down in mid-flight, as if someone had the ball on a string and jerked it

The curve ball is thrown by holding the first two fingers close together along one of the seams *(see above)*. As the pitcher gets near the end of the delivery, the pitcher snaps his or her wrist to put a spin on the ball. The spin causes the ball to move in flight. Throwing a curve ball should not strain the pitcher's arm.

New York Yankee Mariano Rivera, one of the greatest closers in baseball, throws his famous "cut" fastball while a runner lurks on third base.

In the outfield

The greatest outfielders know the importance of the strategy of the position—hitting the cutoff man, throwing to the right player in a given situation, anticipating the strength of the hitter. A champion wins games not only at the plate but by playing defense in the field. A good throw to the plate is as important as a home run.

Strategy

Outfielders are roamers. They sprint from one spot to another. Even when the ball is hit in the infield, the outfielder must back up the fielder in case the ball takes a bad bounce or skips by the infielder.

Outfield play also requires strategy. Outfielders must have a good jump on the ball. They should recognize what kind of hitter is at the plate— a power hitter? A singles hitter? An outfielder should also know whether the count favors the hitter and whether the pitcher often gives up fly balls.

A skillful outfielder will have good range. Good range means a player is fast and has good judgment about where a ball is going to land. He can cover much more space and chase down many more fly balls than a player with limited range.

After a base hit into the outfield, the outfielder must throw accurately to an infielder—called the cutoff man. The outfielder should make sure to throw the ball to his or her glove above his or her head. The cutoff man can redirect the ball to cut off a runner trying to advance on the basepaths.

A spectacular defensive play is as important as a home run—this outfielder leaps to make a catch in centerfield.

"The Catch"

During the World Series in September 1954, Willie Mays ran down and caught a baseball hit 450 feet. It is remembered simply as "The Catch," one of the greatest defensive plays in baseball history. Mays recalled what was going through his mind as he made the play.

"I saw it cleanly. As soon as I picked it out of the sky, I knew I had to get toward centerfield. I turned and ran at full speed toward center with my back to the plate. But even as I was running I realized I had to be in stride if I was going to catch it, so about 450 feet away from the plate I looked up over my left shoulder and could see the ball. I timed it perfectly and it dropped into my glove maybe ten or fifteen feet from the bleacher wall."

Mays threw the ball quickly back to the infield, saving a run. Inspired by the catch, Mays and the Giants went on to win the World Series.

Andruw Jones, one of the best center fielders in the sport today, makes this catch look easy.

In the infield

Infielders, except for first base, must be extremely fast and agile. They face hard skipping ground balls, high pop up fly balls, and screaming line drives. The infielder must be ready to jump this way and that, adjusting in a split second to position themselves to best make the play.

Positioning

The infielder should be positioned properly for each hitter. A few inches and one step can mean the difference between a base hit and an out.

A good infielder will know what pitch his pitcher will throw in a given situation. This allows him to set up for the most likely ball. Certain pitches will most likely be hit on the ground or in the air. The infielder must also know opposing hitters, their tendencies, and their strengths. He or she will know if the hitter is strong enough to muscle the ball into the outfield or shoot a ground ball up the middle.

Hall of Famer and Gold Glove shortstop Cal Ripken Jr. knew the importance of positioning before the ball was hit. Ripken also knew each batter and where they were most likely to hit the ball—whether they would pull it or slap it up the middle. This kind of thinking meant Ripken did not have to cover as much ground to reach a ball—he was already there. "I get a kick when a guy says to me after a play, 'How the heck did you get to that ball?'" Ripken wrote.

Masters of adjustment

Infield defensive play can save or lose a game. A good infielder will rob hits, turn double plays that appear impossible, and make powerful throws from the cutoff position to beat runners sliding into home. The greatest infielders can adjust to anything hit or thrown at them.

This Atlanta Brave infielder is set to scoop up a ground ball and make an out.

Derek Jeter

Derek Jeter, the New York Yankees shortstop, wanted few things out of life: to play baseball, to play shortstop, and to play for the Yankees. His father had been a shortstop, and he hoped to follow the example set by his dad. It was not easy in the beginning. Jeter, who has a career .317 batting average, recalled his first season in the minor leagues at shortstop, where he made a whopping 56 errors. "I probably cried once about each error. Cried to my parents and cried myself to sleep. Man that was difficult," he recalled.

The unassisted triple play

The unassisted triple play is when a single fielder makes three outs without any help. Only twelve have been made in baseball history. The last one, on August 10, 2003, was made by shortstop Rafael Furcal of the Atlanta Braves. With runners on first and second in the fifth inning, Furcal made a leaping grab of St. Louis Cardinal Woody Williams's line drive. The runners had been running on the pitch, and Furcal stepped on second base to double up Mike Matheny. Furcal then tagged out Orlando Palmeiro as he tried to run back to first.

Catching

The catcher is a critically important defensive position. From the catcher's position behind the plate, he or she can see the entire game unfold. The catcher directs the defense, guides pitchers, and makes crucial tags at the plate.

In every play

The catcher squats behind home plate and is a part of every play. The catcher is a balance of brain and brawn. He or she researches batters, suggests what pitch is best in each situation, and uses conversation and body language to keep the pitcher focused. During play, the catcher must be able to block breaking balls that drop into the dirt, throw out base runners, and run down pop flies behind the plate.

Catchers must keep their poise and make the tag on a hard-charging runner. In the 2003 NLDS, San Francisco catcher Benito Santiago tags out Florida Marlin Lenny Harris when Harris tries to score on a fly ball.

When the ball is hit into the infield, the catcher often directs which player should field it. When a runner slides into home plate, the catcher must snag the throw, make the tag, and keep his or her nerve as the player runs into him or her.

Guiding the pitcher

The catcher is critically important to the pitcher. It is the catcher's job to research opposing hitters and call pitches. The catcher also acts as a coach and uses mound chats to keep the pitcher focused to encourage him or her if the game is going poorly.

Hall of Fame catcher Yogi Berra of the New York Yankees brought a sense of humor to catching and to baseball. Berra worked hard to establish a good relationship with his pitchers. During a tense situation in a game, he walked to the mound and loosened up his pitcher with a few jokes. He also offered good advice about how to pitch to the next hitter or what to do next. "You tell people what you want done, even if they know it perfectly well," wrote Berra. "Reminders can't hurt. You write memoirs or letters or e-mails, you have meetings, discuss goals. It's all about communication."

Catchers are so important that some pitchers will only work with certain catchers. They like the catcher's pitch selection and they believe his or her defensive skills match up well with the types of pitches they throw.

Many teams build their entire strategy around their catcher. Some teams want a catcher who can hit, and they will accept it if his defense is not perfect. Others believe a catcher's most important job is behind the plate, making defensive plays and calling pitches. They accept that the catcher will probably hit poorly.

Communication is essential. Here, Jorge Posada talks over a pitch with David Wells.

Baserunning

Baserunning requires speed and good judgment. A baserunner must be able to make quick decisions and accurately judge the strength of a catcher or outfielder's arm. Baserunners also steal bases, using it as a weapon to unnerve an opposing pitcher and make the defense tense. The best baserunners have heart, daring, and brains. They get the most out of every hit and take advantage of each defensive mistake.

Body language

A baseball star is always observing, seeking clues from the other players around him through body language, unconscious gestures, and patterns. They best use this against their opponents. They calculate exactly when the pitcher is going to throw home and when he or she is going to attempt a pickoff move. They know if the catcher has a weak or a strong arm.

The all-time steal record

Ricky Henderson presently holds the all-time record for most steals with 1,406. In 1982, he stole 130 times, more than many entire teams steal all season. In the final game of the season, he stole three bases, including two in one inning! The tally is the single-season record for most steals.

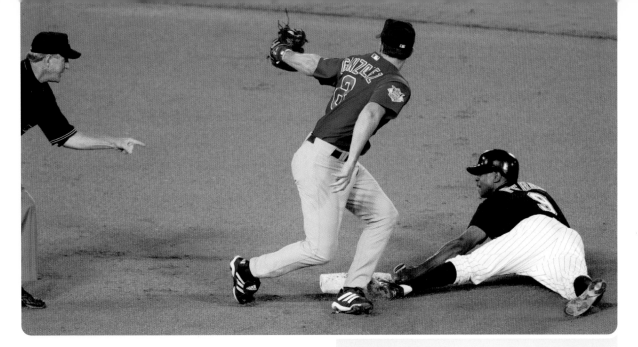

Did he make it? After the runner has slid into second, both the runner and the fielder look to the umpire for the call.

Moreover, the best players store this information away, waiting for the exact moment to spring it on the opposing team.

Psychology

One of the greatest baserunners of all time was Ty Cobb, who played in the early 1900s for the Detroit Tigers. Cobb called baserunning "waging war on the basepaths." He gave advice to many young players about baseball, especially what to do to win games through baserunning. "Train yourself, boys, to think along psychological lines," wrote Cobb. "Even big leaguers are a bundle of nerves when a game is close, and there are untold ways when running the bases of using that to your advantage."

Cobb devised a strategy when he was sliding into second or third to beat a throw. He focused on the body language of the fielder over the bag. By watching the fielder, Cobb could spot where the ball was going to land. He used one of eight different types of slides to beat the tag.

Some fielders, Cobb noted, were smarter. They didn't give away with their body movements where the ball was going to land. So Cobb learned to ignore their bodies and instead concentrate on their eyes. Cobb watched the fielders watch the ball, thus giving away where it was going. After a dirty slide, Cobb was usually safe.

The double steal fact

When baserunners are on first and second, the manager may call for the double steal. The double steal occurs when both runners take off at the same time for second and third. It is a dramatic but risky play. The catcher only has to throw 90 feet to catch a runner at third. If it works, however, a base hit could score two runs.

Coaching

The manager and coaches form the backbone of each baseball team. The manager makes the lineup, encourages or criticizes players, and makes calls during a game that often determine victory or defeat. A great manager must be a teacher, a master of baseball strategy, and a student of human nature. He or she must do the little things to get the best out of his or her coaches and players.

Preparation and practice

A manager must get his players physically and mentally ready to play each game. The first requires good organization and preparation. Managers must have a schedule for practices that will not waste time. The manager must also coordinate various activities at once, since baseball requires specialized skills.

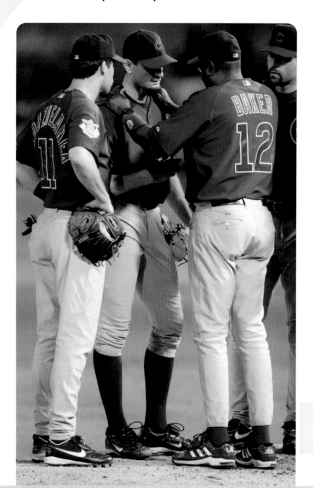

While one player hits in the batting cage, others should be practicing defensive plays or learning strategy. The worst thing in a practice is to have a group of players standing around and watching other players practice.

Coaches

Most baseball teams have an assistant manager or coaches that specialize in batting or pitching. These coaches are extremely valuable. While the manager directs a practice, they can focus on individual coaching sessions and teach small techniques and adjustments—such as a batting stance or a pitcher's wind up.

During a game, base coaches help baserunners on the basepaths. The first base coach will tell a runner about the pitcher's pickoff moves. The third base coach is essential in directing a runner to continue running to home or stop at third after a hit.

The right attitude

Most Major League baseball players began their careers in a youth league. Though they experienced

Dusty Baker, manager of the Chicago Cubs, talks to pitcher Matt Clement during the 2003 NLCS in Florida.

George "Sparky" Anderson

George "Sparky" Anderson managed in the Major Leagues for 27 years, first for the Cincinnati Reds and then for the Detroit Tigers. He won the World Series with the Reds in 1975 and 1976 and with the Tigers in 1984. Twenty-seven years is a long time to deal with the pressure of managing Major League players and dealing with reporters and fans. Still, Anderson was always enthusiastic. Why? "I give three reasons," he said. "One, my love for the game. Two, the enjoyment and satisfaction of working with players. And three, the competition each season to be the best." Anderson called the ballpark his "office," and he urged coaches to be as organized as the leader of any successful company.

many different coaches and quality of play, they all agree that a good coach creates an atmosphere of competition and fun. Young players will not reach their potential if they are not enjoying themselves.

Coaches who have won and lost the most

The coaches with the best records often also have the worst ones as well. Connie Mack managed his teams to 3,948 losses, the most in baseball history. Casey Stengel, a legendary manager, lost 1,842 games. Manager Tony LaRussa of the St. Louis Cardinals has lost more than 1,700 games. Which managers have won the most games? Connie Mack, with 3,731 wins. Casey Stengel is ninth on the all-time list, leading his team to 1,905 wins. Tony LaRussa has won more than 1,900.

Tony LaRussa argues with home plate umpire Mike Winters after being thrown out of the game for arguing a strike call.

Fitness

Keeping physically fit and building up strength is important in any sport, but baseball requires a special approach. Warm-up is absolutely essential or an injury can cut short a season or even a career. Young players should be very careful about weight training. Too many large muscles can actually make it harder to perfect the delicate movements one needs to compete in baseball.

All great baseball players spend time warming up and preparing their bodies for play. Baseball is a game of starts and stops. A player can spend several minutes sitting on a bench or standing in the field and then suddenly be expected to sprint, twist, and throw. These kinds of rapid and sudden movements put enormous stress on joints and muscles. The body must be ready.

Atlanta Braves scout and former pitcher John Stewart said preparation before a game was absolutely critical. "Warm up for a pitcher is probably the most important aspect of the game," he wrote. "Without it, injury is nearly guaranteed."

Derek Jeter stretches his legs before a game. If he does not stretch, he is far more likely to be injured.

Consecutive game records fact

Some players rarely ever miss a game, even over several seasons. Cal Ripken Jr. played 2,632 games in a row. New York Yankee Lou Gehrig, who played his first game on June 1, 1925, played 2,130 straight games. Steve Garvey, who spent most of his career with Los Angeles Dodgers in the 1970s and 1980s, played 1,207 straight games.

Nolan Ryan

Pitcher Nolan Ryan was a fanatic about keeping his arm healthy—and it showed. He pitched into his early 40s and was voted into the Hall of Fame. He urged players to listen to their bodies when training. "I don't believe in the no-pain, no-gain philosophy of weight training. If you're doing a specific exercise and you experience pain, stop; your body is trying to tell you something," said Ryan. Ryan explained that there are two kinds of pain. There's the normal stiffness after a long workout. Muscles may ache the next morning. This discomfort usually fades at the beginning of the next workout. Sharp pain that increases, however, should not be ignored.

The right diet

Any successful baseball player has a balanced diet that includes carbohydrates, fats, and proteins. Pasta is a popular dish to keep a player's energy level high. Baseball games typically last two to three hours each and are often played in hot and humid weather. A player should keep himself hydrated with fluids throughout the day. Drinking too much just before a game, however, causes more problems than it solves.

Weight training

Weight training should be done with caution. For a long time, baseball players avoided it because it could upset the delicate fluid motions players need to make plays. A classic example of this effect was Jose Canseco. Canseco, who had his best seasons with the Oakland A's in the 1980s, could hit with power, but he could also run the bases. Then Canseco lifted weights and bulked up. His play in the field suffered, and he could no longer run as fast. He soon became a designated hitter (DH) whose only job was to hit home runs.

Injuries

Baseball makes enormous demands on the body's joints. The repetitive motion of swinging a bat or throwing a baseball can tear cartilage and muscles. The explosive speed and power required by the sport can do the same. Jarring collisions, slides, and getting hit by the ball, can bruise or even break a bone.

Another common pitcher's injury is the torn rotator cuff. This tear occurs to one of the muscle groups in the shoulder. This injury can be devastating, because a shoulder injury makes the entire arm useless.

Pitching out of a wind up puts enormous strain on several muscles, most of them not in the arm. The back and legs are just as essential to pitching, and top players will pay attention to keeping them strong and healthy. If these muscles are injured and the pitcher's arm is fine, he or she will still be unable to pitch.

Pitchers

Pitchers are among the most vulnerable to injuries. Though they throw only once every several games, they must exert their full energy on each pitch. Many pitchers also try too hard, either in the game or in practice, tearing tissue. Unless the pitcher agrees to stop playing, which few want to do, the tear will only get worse and could threaten a career.

The elbow is commonly a problem for pitchers. Over several years, pieces of bone can break off from the elbow and float in the socket, causing pitchers great pain. Most pitchers have surgery to repair it.

Tommy John surgery

Tommy John, a pitcher in the 1970s and 1980s, tore a ligament in his elbow. Surgery rebuilt the tissue in his elbow, which allowed him to come back throwing stronger than before. This procedure, now called Tommy John surgery, has saved many pitcher's careers. Some pitchers have even had the surgery when the injury was not so serious because they hoped to add power to their fastball.

Ken Griffey Jr. struggled with injuries later in his career.

Avoiding injury

A rule of thumb for players about injuries is that if the pain goes away after warm up, it is probably not serious. If the pain increases, however, the player should stop immediately.

Leo Mazzone urged players to tell their coach. "If you are pitching and you know you're getting tired, don't be afraid to let your coach in on it. Don't keep it a secret and hurt your team," he said.

Players in the field can get injured by playing on a poorly tended field. Yankee legend Mickey Mantle tore ligaments in his knee in a game when he tripped over a drainage pipe. The injury plagued him for the rest of his career. Other injuries are usually pulled muscles. To treat these as well as bruises, the player should use cold packs or heat compresses. The top players know that injuries are best avoided in the first place by stretching and warming up.

Baseball is sometimes a contact sport, and that can cause bumps and bruises. Treat these injuries quickly, so they don't become a problem later.

Baseball strategies and plays

Baseball players and coaches have developed special plays and strategies, some of which are described below. Each young player should know about these plays and be prepared to either make them, or know how to deal with them.

The hit and run

The "hit and run" is a play for when there is a runner on first base (runners can also be on first and second) and the hitter is at a "hitter's count." A hitter's count is more than two balls and less than two strikes, eg: 2-1; 3-1. In that situation, the pitcher is usually trying to throw a strike. The hitter is instructed to make contact on the next pitch, while the runner sprints toward second base, opening a hole when the second baseman or shortstop covers second base. In a perfect hit and run, the hitter grounds a ball through the hole. The double play is avoided and runners will be at first and third, a favorable situation to score runs.

The squeeze

The "squeeze play" is called when there is a runner on third and less than one out. The hitter is told to lay down a bunt, which allows the runner to score from third. A "suicide squeeze" calls for the runner to break from third when the pitcher releases the ball. It is almost a guaranteed run if the hitter makes a successful bunt. If, however, the hitter does not make contact, then the runner is almost always tagged out. That is why it is called a suicide squeeze.

Defensive strategy

Strategies and plays are not just for the offense, but for the defense as well. Coaches often bring in relief pitchers late in the game or in special situations. The coach tries to match the pitching arm with the opposing hitter. Facing a lefty batter, the coach will call in a lefty pitcher. The coach will match a right-handed batter with a right-handed

This batter has just made a bunt, which can be an important technique to advance runners.

The defensive shift

The entire infield defense can "shift" for certain batters. When a very good left-handed hitter comes to the plate, such as New York Yankee Jason Giambi, the infielders will move to their left. This is because Giambi is far more likely to hit the ball in that direction. The first baseman played behind first base on the line, the second baseman played where the first baseman usually played, the shortstop played near second base, and the third baseman played where the shortstop played. Third base is left open. This is a special defense only used once in a while. But it can rob a batter of hits down the first base line and up the middle.

pitcher. Pitchers have an advantage pitching against a batter that bats from the same side. The ball is harder for the hitter to spot and adjust to.

The Boston Red Sox infield is shifted—meaning they are all playing on the right side of the infield.

With less than two outs and a runner on third, the coach will often order the infield to play closer in, or on the lip of the grass of the infield. The intention is to make it impossible for the runner on third to score on a ground ball. This strategy does have drawbacks, however. The infielders have less range, and a hard hit ball between the fielders almost always goes through for a base hit.

Working on skills

Baseball is a sport of repetition, and working on skills means practicing drills over and over again. There are different drills suited for each position.

The long toss

Throwing is something every baseball player needs to do. To build up arm strength, players practice the long toss. Starting at a short distance, they throw to a partner. After each throw, they take a step back. The throws will get longer, demanding more power and accuracy. Done over several weeks, this drill will strengthen the throwing arm.

Pitcher Ila Borders prepares to throw a pitch in a game against the Sioux Falls Canaries. She pitched six shut-out innings, leading her team to victory and making her the first woman to win a minor league baseball game.

In the infield

Infielders can practice short-hops and ground balls. A partner can roll the ball to the infielder's side, alternating back and forth. The infielder will learn how to increase his or her range and field balls. To field, the infielder should be low to the ground, knees bent, leaning forward on the balls of their feet. The knees should be bent, not the waist. This position allows the fielder to move quickly in any direction.

The glove should be held forward so the infielder can see the ball easily. When the ball is streaking through the infield, the infielder must make tiny adjustments to ensure it lands correctly in the glove. The best infielders give slightly, using "soft hands" to absorb the spin and velocity of a hard hit ball. They start with the glove low to the ground and move up to intercept it. They never lower the glove to catch the ball, which is difficult and will slow the throw.

Practice, of course, makes perfect. A good infielder will have taken thousands of ground balls. A young player should not begin training on a rutted or pockmarked field which is common in early spring in areas with cold winters. It is very difficult to develop the hand-eye coordination necessary for the infield when every other ball has a bad hop.

The batting cage is where hitters take pitches for hours and work on their swing.

In the outfield

Good outfield play also requires drills. To develop their ability to run down difficult fly balls, outfielders can get a friend to hit wiffle balls into the air with a tennis racket. The friend should aim the balls to land behind the outfielder's head. This drill teaches outfielders how to read fly balls and the footwork necessary to get into position. Outfielders should also catch fly balls hit from a batter as often as they can. Nothing substitutes for running down fly balls over and over again.

This young player holds the bat properly and is concentrating on the next pitch.

Knowing the game

Top players will learn the rhythms of baseball and study opponents to find their weaknesses. Baseball games are won and lost by these observations.

Reading the order

Top players will size up an opposing hitter by checking his or her spot in the batting order. The lead-off and second hitters tend to be fast and make good contact. They rarely hit home runs but they also rarely strike out. The third hitter should hit for high average and power. He or she hopes to get a hit and score the first and second hitters. The fourth batter is a power hitter. He or she hits it far, but also strikes out more. The fifth batter is the heart of the order. He or she is more of a combination of a power and contact hitter. The lower half of the order tends to have weaker hitters. They can hit for power or contact, but are usually arranged in descending skill level to the ninth hitter.

Outfielders— strengths and weaknesses

Young players should also know the opposing defense. The rightfielder tends to have the best arm, because he or she must throw out runners at

Here, veteran pitcher Kenny Rogers takes time to explain a pitching concept to a younger player.

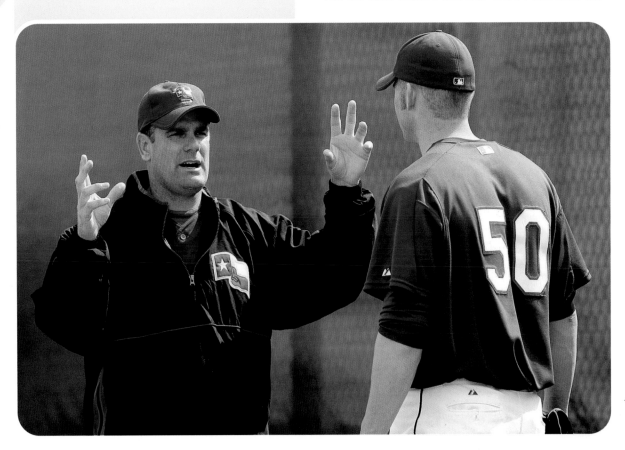

third base. The centerfielder has the best range and the surest glove. The leftfielder usually has the weakest arm. However, since so many players are right handed in Little League and high school, rightfielders have sometimes the least skilled arm and glove. They have the least chance of actually fielding a ball. The top player will watch him or her carefully during practice to find out. If the player is on first and a ball is singled into right field, he or she may be able to beat the fielder's throw to third.

What kind of pitcher?

Top players will ask themselves questions about the opposing pitcher. Does he or she throw fastballs or breaking balls? Does he or she get nervous after falling behind in the count? How does he or she start hitters off? When players have these answers, they can plan the next at bat to take advantage of the pitcher's weaknesses.

A good time to watch an opposing batter is to study them as they hit in the batting cage.

Unwritten rules

A good baseball player will be familiar with some unwritten rules of baseball. The first or third out should never be made at third base. Runners should stay on second and give their teammates the chance to bat a run in. Batters should try to advance the runners over. When a runner is on second with no outs, a good player will hit to the right side of the field to advance the runner to third, where he can be scored on a sacrifice fly.

On defense, the fielder always tries to get the lead runner out. That keeps runners out of scoring position and maintains the force play at other bases.

The World Series

Every fall, all eyes of the baseball world turn to the sport's greatest final—the World Series. It is a grueling series, which pits the best team from the American League against the best team from the National League. The teams have excelled through a 162-game season and two rounds of playoffs. The World Series has given baseball some of its most memorable moments and drama.

Bill Buckner

In the tenth inning of Game Six of the 1986 World Series, the Boston Red Sox, who have not won the World Series since 1918, led by two runs. The New York Mets, however, were not finished. They clawed back and scored two runs. With a runner on second, Mookie Wilson dribbled a ground ball down the first base line. First baseman Bill Buckner hustled to the ball, reached down, and it skipped through his legs. The Mets and their fans rejoiced and went on to win the series the next day. Boston's hopes were crushed again.

Kirby Puckett

In the 1991 World Series, the Atlanta Braves held a three to two game lead over the Minnesota Twins. In Game Six, Kirby Puckett of the Twins had one of the greatest individual performances in World Series history. He had an RBI triple in the first inning, a memorable leaping catch in the third, a go-ahead sacrifice fly in the fifth, and a single and stolen base in the eighth. As if that were not enough, Puckett stepped into the batter's box in the eleventh inning with the score tied 3-3. He slammed

1991 World Series

The 1991 World Series between the Minnesota Twins and the Atlanta Braves is sometimes called the greatest World Series in baseball history. The pitching and defense were superb. Five games were decided by one run, four games decided in the last at-bat, and three in extra-inning games. Game 7 was probably the greatest World Series pitchers' duel of all time. Jack Morris of the Twins pitched ten shut-out innings and allowed only seven hits to beat John Smoltz of the Braves 1-0.

Luis Gonzalez hits a soft line drive which sailed over the Yankee infielders' heads, that drove in the winning run of the 2001 World Series.

the fourth pitch into the left field bleachers. The Twins went on to win the seventh game and captured the World Series title.

2001

In 2001, the New York Yankees and Arizona Diamondbacks were tied three games each. In the final game, the Yankees led 2–1 going into the bottom of the ninth. The Diamondbacks faced the Yankees ace closer Mariano Rivera, then regarded as the best closer in the game. The Diamondback batters, however, were patient. When Rivera made a fielding error, they had runners at first and third with one out. To prevent a score on a ground ball, the Yankees infielders were forced to play in close on the grass. Luis Gonzalez came to bat and hit a soft line drive over the Yankee infielders, scoring a run and winning the game.

Yankees fact

The first World Series was held in 1903. Since then, the Yankees have played in 38 of them and won 26. The closest competitors are the Oakland A's and the St. Louis Cardinals, who have won nine World Series each. No other Major League baseball team comes close to the Yankees' accomplishment. For this reason, the Yankees are traditionally the most loved, and most hated, team in baseball.

Life of a baseball star

Professional baseball players make enormous amounts of money playing a game, but it is not always fun and easy. They play virtually every day for several months a year, and they must deal with thousands of people watching and judging them every time they take the field. Baseball players make enormous amounts of money but must learn to deal with fame. Normal routines, such as going to a movie theater or restaurant, can be disrupted by autograph seekers. The baseball star has to cope with this as well as enjoy playing professional baseball.

A grueling schedule

Baseball is played almost every day over a 162-game season. The best teams then face three levels of playoffs. This schedule is exhausting, with hours spent on buses and airplanes and days or weeks spent away from home and family.

Baseball is also demanding as a culture. Playing every day means preparing every day. It means

Ichiro Suzuki of the Seattle Mariners faces a wall of autograph seekers. Professional baseball players often spend hours signing items for fans.

Barry Bonds

San Francisco Giant Barry Bonds has been baseball's greatest hitter through the late 1990s and early 2000s. Besides being voted MVP six times, Bonds holds the single season home run record of 73 and had hit 658 home runs by the end of the 2003 season. Bonds appears within striking distance of the all-time home run record of 755 held by Henry "Hank" Aaron.

ignoring minor pain caused by tired muscles and light bruises. Most players have tough work ethics and hour-long routines they use to get prepared to play.

Baseball players, of course, make a lot of money. In 2003, the average Major-League salary was $2.56 million per year. The high salaries have also caused problems, enraging commentators who call the players greedy and spoiled. It has also caused an enormous gap between the players and fans, most of whom will not make $2.56 million in an entire lifetime.

In the spotlight

Some players take the pressure and attention of fame in stride. Alex Rodriguez, the highest paid baseball player ever, took writing classes in the off-season at a community college in Miami. No one in the class, including the professor, recognized him. Then the professor asked everyone to say a little about themselves. When Rodriguez mentioned that he had traveled to virtually every city in North America as a baseball player, his classmates realized who he was. "After that," he recalled, "they brought posters or balls in for me to sign, but I was still able to fit in."

Records

Baseball is a game of statistics. Fans pore over them, calculating which player has done better and why. Listed below are some of the most common baseball statistics. Home Runs measure power —which player has hit the ball the most times over the fence. Strike outs measure a pitcher's effectiveness—how many times he has used his skills and strength to make a batter swing and miss for strike three. Steals measure speed and intelligence. Hits are a good measure of a batter's ability. Statistics are up to the 2003 season.

Career Home Run Leaders Since 1900		
Name	Date	Runs
1 Hank Aaron	(1954–1974)	755
2 Babe Ruth	(1914–1935)	714
3 Willie Mays	(1951–1972)	660
4 Barry Bonds	(1986–)	658
5 Frank Robinson	(1956–1976)	586

Lifetime Batting Average Since 1900		
Name	Date	Average
1 Ty Cobb	(1905–1928)	.367
2 Rogers Hornsby	(1915–1937)	.358
3 Ed Delahanty	(1888–1903)	.346
4 Tris Speaker	(1907–1928)	.345
5 Ted Williams	(1939–1960)	.345

Lifetime Hits Leaders Since 1900		
Name	Date	Wins
1 Pete Rose	(1963–1986)	4,256
2 Ty Cobb	(1905–1928)	4,189
3 Hank Aaron	(1954–1976)	3,771
4 Stan Musial	(1941–1963)	3,630
5 Tris Speaker	(1907–1928)	3,514

Pitching wins		
Name	Date	Wins
1 Cy Young	(1890–1911)	511
2 Walter Johnson	(1907–1927)	417
3= Pete Alexander	(1911–1930)	373
3= Christy Mathewson	(1900–1906)	373

World Series Winners 1978–2003	
Name	Date
Florida Marlins	2003
Anaheim Angels	2002
Arizona Diamondbacks	2001
New York Yankees	2000
New York Yankees	1999
New York Yankees	1998
Florida Marlins	1997
New York Yankees	1996
Atlanta Braves	1995
Not held due to players' strike	1994
Toronto Blue Jays	1993
Toronto Blue Jays	1992
Minnesota Twins	1991
Cincinnati Reds	1990
Oakland A's	1989
Los Angeles Dodgers	1988
Minnesota Twins	1987
New York Mets	1986
Kansas City Royals	1985
Detroit Tigers	1984
Baltimore Orioles	1983
St. Louis Cardinals	1982
Los Angeles Dodgers	1981
Philadelphia Phillies	1980
Pittsburgh Pirates	1979
New York Yankees	1978

Breaking Babe Ruth's home run record

Another record many believed would not be broken was Babe Ruth's all-time home run tally of 714. Atlanta Brave Hank Aaron, however, closed in. On April 8, 1974, he hit his 715th, shattering Ruth's record and driving the Atlanta fans into a frenzy. As he rounded the bases, he shook hands with three of the Dodger infielders and crossed the plate. Aaron finished his career with 755 home runs, a record many now insist will never be broken.

Lifetime Earned Run Average (ERA) Since 1900		
Name	Date	ERA
1 Ed Walsh	(1904–1917)	1.82
2 Addie Joss	(1902–1910)	1.89
3 Mordecai Brown	(1903–1916)	2.06

Career Strikeouts Since 1900		
Name	Date	Strikeouts
1 Nolan Ryan	(1966–1993)	5,714
2 Steve Carlton	(1965–1988)	4,136
3 Roger Clemens	(1984–)	4,099
4 Randy Johnson	(1988–)	3,871
5 Bert Blyleven	(1970–1992)	3,701

Glossary

agile nimble, quick

backspin when the ball is spinning backwards

batting average the percentage that indicates how many times a batter has gotten a hit, out of the times he has batted

breaking ball or breaking pitch a pitch that weaves, bobs, or slides.

bunt to bat a ball lightly so it rolls into the infield

carbohydrate a fundamental part of food formed largely from starch, Pasta is high in carbohydrates

cartilage rubbery, tough elastic tissue

change-up a pitch that is thrown like a fastball but is slower. The "change-up" is designed to confuse the batter and upset their timing.

closer relief pitcher brought in to pitch to the last batter (or batters)

cricket English game in which a player attempts to throw or "bowl" a ball past an opposing batter

cutoff man the infielder who moves into the shallow area of the outfield during a base hit. He takes the throw from the outfielder.

double play when two outs are made in one play

draft when a sports team takes exclusive rights to a young player to play for their team

durable able to withstand use and wear

fastball a pitch thrown to overwhelm the batter with speed and location

fatigue wear-and-tear, exhaustion

force play where baserunner is out because he must get to a base

hydrated a state of having drunk a sufficient amount of water

infield area of baseball field that stretches from home plate outward, past the pitcher's mound, and includes the dirt around first, second, and third. Also the players who field in this area.

line drive a ball hit off the ground in a straight line

lineup a list of the players who will play on game day

MVP most valuable player, each league votes one player MVP after each season

pickoff a move in which a pitcher or catcher tries to throw out a baserunner between pitches

pitch selection the strategy a catcher and pitcher use to pitch to a batter

prospect a player who shows great potential for future play

RBI "runs batted in" this statistic counts how many times a batter has scored other runners with his hits. It shows a player's effectiveness when runners are in scoring position

regulations the rules by which a sport is played

rounders old English game similar to baseball

sacrifice when a batter deliberately makes an out to advance a runner

scoring position when a player is on a base, second or third, where he can be scored by a single

scout a person who observes players to determine their strengths and weaknesses

shut out where the opposing team scores no runs

slide when a baserunner dives to beat a throw at a base

stance the posture and position of the batter at the plate

wind up a pitcher's motion to throw to the plate

Resources

Major baseball organizations

Little League Baseball International
P.O. Box 3485
Williamsport, PA 17701
570-326-1921

Babe Ruth League
International Headquarters
1770 Brunswick Pike
Trenton, NJ 08638
609-695-1434

Major League Baseball
The Office of the Commissioner of Baseball
245 Park Avenue, 31st Floor
New York, NY 10167
212-931-7800

USA Baseball
P.O. Box 1131
Durham, NC 27702
919-474-8721

* To find an organization's website, use a search engine and type in the organization's name as a keyword.

Further reading

Christopher, Matt. *Matt Christopher's Great Moments in Baseball History*. New York City: Little Brown & Company, 1996.

Johnson, Randy and Rosenthal, Jim. *Randy Johnson's Power Pitching: The Big Unit's Secrets to Domination, Intimidation, and Winning*. New York City: Three Rivers Press, 2003.

Kelley, James. *Eyewitness: Baseball*. New York City: DK Publishing, 2000.

Monteleone, John. *Little League Baseball Guide to Correcting the 25 Most Common Mistakes*. Chicago: McGraw-Hill Books, 2003.

Morgan, Joe and Lally, Richard. *Baseball for Dummies*. New York: Wiley Publishing Ltd., 2000.

Index